MARIACHI

Sierra Wilson

MY FAVORITE MUSIC

AV2

www.openlightbox.com

AV2

Step 1
Go to **www.openlightbox.com**

Step 2
Enter this unique code
RLMIO7O2Y

Step 3
Explore your interactive eBook!

AV2 is optimized for use on any device

Your interactive eBook comes with...

- **Read — Audio**: Listen to the entire book read aloud
- **Videos**: Watch informative video clips
- **Weblinks**: Gain additional information for research
- **Try This!**: Complete activities and hands-on experiments
- **Key Words**: Study vocabulary, and complete a matching word activity
- **Quizzes**: Test your knowledge
- **Slideshows**: View images and captions
- **Share**: Share titles within your Learning Management System (LMS) or Library Circulation System
- **Citation**: Create bibliographical references following APA, CMOS, and MLA styles

This title is part of our AV2 digital subscription

1-Year K–5 Subscription
ISBN 978-1-7911-3320-7

Access hundreds of AV2 titles with our digital subscription.
Sign up for a FREE trial at **www.openlightbox.com/trial**

The digital components of this book are guaranteed to stay active for at least five years from the date of publication.

MARIACHI

Contents

I love music.

Mariachi is my favorite kind of music.

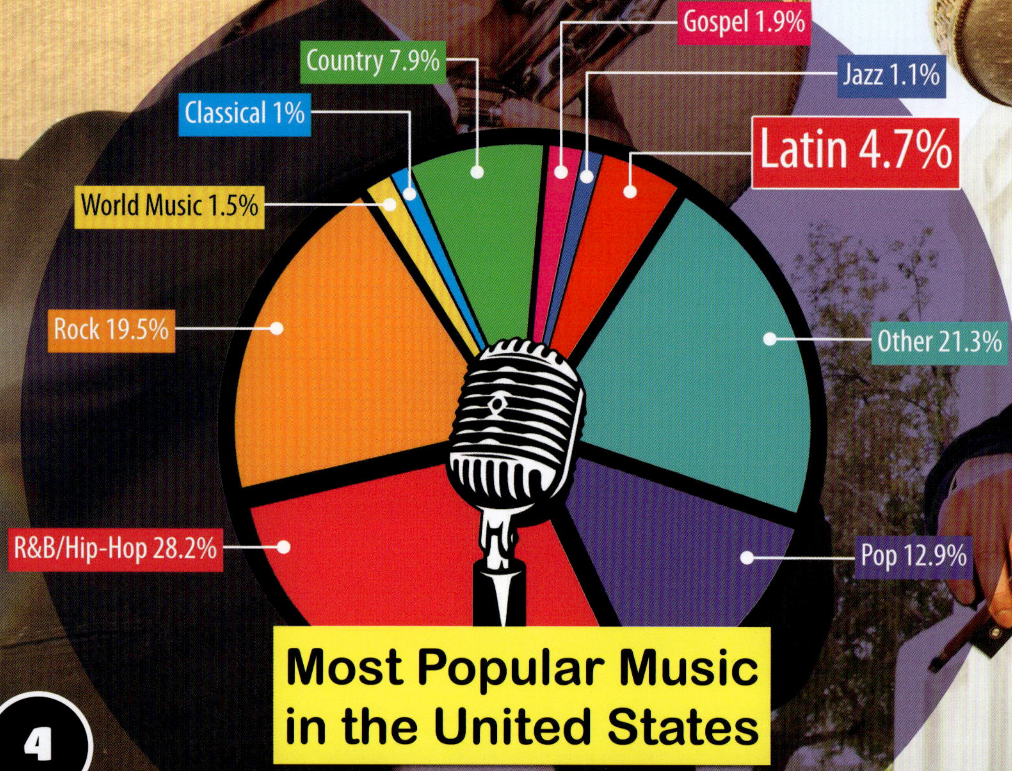

Mariachi music comes from western Mexico. It started in the late 1700s.

Mexican farm workers were the first people to play mariachi music.

They played mariachi at parties called fiestas.

The first mariachi music was played using string instruments.

Over time, trumpets and other instruments were added.

Mariachi singers usually sing in Spanish.

Their voices are strong and full of emotion.

Mariachi songs often tell stories about life in Mexico.

Many mariachi songs are about love and heartbreak.

String instruments and trumpets are still the main mariachi instruments.

Some of today's mariachi bands also have an accordion.

I like to play mariachi music with my friends.

Each person sings and plays a different instrument.

Playing in a band teaches us how to work together.

Guadalajara, Mexico, is home to the world's largest mariachi festival.

More than 2 million people go to the festival every year.

I love mariachi music.

It teaches me about love and life.

MARIACHI FACTS

These pages provide detailed information that expands on the interesting facts found in the book. They are intended to be used by adults as a learning support to help young readers round out their knowledge of each musical genre featured in the *My Favorite Music* series.

Pages 4–5

I love music. Mariachi music is my favorite kind of music. Music is the name given to sounds made with voices or musical instruments and put together in a way that conveys emotion. People use music to express themselves. Mariachi is one of the most popular forms of music in Mexico. It is also well-known in the United States and other countries. Mariachi is so important to Mexican culture that it has been designated as a UNESCO Intangible Cultural Heritage. This designation indicates that it must be saved for future generations.

Pages 6–7

Mexican farm workers were the first people to play mariachi music. The rhythms and sounds of mariachi reflect Mexico's multicultural history. Musical elements from African, Indigenous, and Spanish music are all a part of mariachi. This type of music first developed in the Jalisco region of Mexico. Farm laborers played it at parties and other special events. It was primarily played to encourage dancing.

Pages 8–9

The first mariachi music was played using string instruments. Common instruments in early mariachi bands included violins and different variations of guitars. One such instrument was the *vihuela*, a small guitar with five strings. Another was the *guitarrón*, a large, six-stringed guitar with a deep bass sound. Some bands also featured the Mexican folk harp. Brass instruments, usually cornets, began to appear in mariachi music in the early 20th century. By the 1930s, trumpets had replaced the cornets.

Pages 10–11

Mariachi singers usually sing in Spanish. As Mexico was colonized by Spain, Spanish has long been the dominant language in the country. Mariachi songs are known for their passion. Singers convey this passion with strong vocals that are full of emotion. Most mariachi singing comes from the chest. This allows for a rich, deep sound. Some songs include vocalizations called *gritos* and *llantos*. *Gritos* are shouting sounds, while *llantos* resemble crying. Both are meant to stress the emotion of the song.

Pages 12–13

Mariachi songs often tell stories about life in Mexico. Mariachi music is versatile. It uses elements from many different styles of music and touches on a variety of themes. One type of song often set to mariachi music is the *ranchera*. A *ranchera* can be fast or slow, with a lyric that discusses rural life, love, or nature. The *corrido* is a ballad that usually focuses on love, historical battles, or brave deeds. Other types of mariachi songs include *boleros* and *jarabes*. There are regional styles of mariachi music as well.

Pages 14–15

String instruments and trumpets are still the main mariachi instruments. Along with the trumpet, the original instruments remain at the core of modern mariachi music. However, some mariachi bands now include other instruments. The accordion is a popular addition, as is the flute. The size of mariachi bands has also changed over time. Initially, mariachi bands had fewer than 10 musicians. Now, some of the bigger bands can have hundreds of performers.

Pages 16–17

I like to play mariachi music with my friends. Creating music with others helps teach children cooperation, teamwork, and how to achieve goals. Children who regularly play music tend to have more confidence and get along better with others. Some students learn better in groups because they do not feel the pressure of having to learn on their own. Mariachi music is fun to play and also allows students to connect with an important cultural heritage.

Pages 18–19

Guadalajara, Mexico, is home to the world's largest mariachi festival. Each summer in Guadalajara, the International Mariachi Festival, or *Encuentro Internacional del Mariachi y la Charrería*, takes place. The festival extends over several days and features a variety of events. This includes a parade and dancing. The main event, however, is watching the world's best mariachi musicians perform in the Teatro Degollado, a theater located in Guadalajara's historic center.

Pages 20–21

I love mariachi music. Recent studies suggest that learning and practicing music can be beneficial to a child's ability to learn. Among these benefits are improved motor skills and dexterity, increased test scores, and even raised Intelligence Quotient, or IQ, scores. Learning music at an early age has also been shown to aid in language development, and to improve reading and listening skills.

SIGHT WORDS

Research has shown that as much as 65 percent of all written material published in English is made up of 300 words. These 300 words cannot be taught using pictures or learned by sounding them out. They must be recognized by sight. This book contains 58 common sight words to help young readers improve their reading fluency and comprehension. This book also teaches young readers several important content words. These words are paired with pictures to aid in learning and improve understanding.

Page	Sight Words First Appearance
4	country, I, in, is, kind, most, my, of, other, states, the, world
5	comes, from, it, late, started
6	farm, first, people, play, to, were
7	at, they
8	was
9	and, over, time
11	are, their
12	about, life, often, songs, tell
13	many
14	still
15	also, an, have, some
16	a, different, each, like, with
17	how, together, us, work
18	home
19	every, go, more, than, year
21	me

Page	Content Words First Appearance
4	classical, gospel, hip-hop, jazz, Latin, mariachi, music, pop, R&B, rock, United States
5	Mexico
6	workers
7	fiestas, parties
8	instruments
9	trumpets
10	singers, Spanish
11	emotion, voices
12	stories
13	heartbreak, love
15	accordion, bands
16	friends, person
18	festival, Guadalajara

Published by Lightbox Learning Inc.
276 5th Avenue, Suite 704 #917
New York, NY 10001
Website: www.openlightbox.com

Library of Congress Cataloging-in-Publication Data
Names: Wilson, Sierra, author.
Title: Mariachi / Sierra Wilson.
Description: New York, NY : Lightbox Learning Inc., 2026. | Series: My favorite music | Audience: Grades 2-3
Identifiers: LCCN 2024058248 (print) | LCCN 2024058249 (ebook) | ISBN 9798874520441 (library binding) | ISBN 9798874520458 (paperback) | ISBN 9798874520465 (ebook other) | ISBN 9798874520472 (ebook other)
Subjects: LCSH: Mariachi--History and criticism--Juvenile literature.
Classification: LCC ML3470 .W674 2025 (print) | LCC ML3470 (ebook) | DDC 782.42164--dc23/eng/20241203
LC record available at https://lccn.loc.gov/2024058248
LC ebook record available at https://lccn.loc.gov/2024058249

Printed in Guangzhou, China
1 2 3 4 5 6 7 8 9 0 29 28 27 26 25

042025
100924

Art Director: Terry Paulhus **Project Coordinator:** Heather Kissock